BRITAIN IN OLD PHOTOGRAPHS

MARLOW
PAST & PRESENT

A. J. (JOCK) CAIRNS

SUTTON PUBLISHING LIMITED

Sutton Publishing Limited
Phoenix Mill · Thrupp · Stroud
Gloucestershire · GL5 2BU

First published 1997

Reprinted in 2002

Cover photographs: *front:* Marlow Rag Regatta,
1926; *back:* munitions workers at Wethered's
Brewery, 1915. *Title page photograph:* Probably
the most photographed feature of Marlow – the
suspension bridge linking Buckinghamshire to
Berkshire and the spire of All Saints' Parish
Church.

British Library Cataloguing in Publication Data
A catalogue record for this book is available from the
British Library.

ISBN 0-7509-1697-4

Typeset in 10/12 Perpetua.
Typesetting and origination by
Sutton Publishing Limited.
Printed in Great Britain by
J.H. Haynes & Co. Ltd, Sparkford.

CONTENTS

Marlow was twinned with Marly-le-Roi, a French town which is virtually a suburb of Paris, in 1972. The following year a civic party from Marlow Urban Council, supported by many associations and clubs, tied the knot on French soil. This picture shows the official ceremony held at la mairie (town hall) that was used by the Gestapo as their local headquarters during the Second World War occupation.

INTRODUCTION

Romans had no interest in the Marlow we know today. There was nothing but a huge lake dominating the area where the town now stands. Their legions sailed and passed by on both sides of it, but left little visible record of their ever having been there. After they left the Saxons started draining the water and gave the area its first name – 'Merlaw'. In Anglo-Saxon this simply meant, 'what is left after draining a mere'. The Normans completed the drainage job and when William I's surveyors arrived twenty years after the Conquest it became known as 'Merlaue'.

But it was not until the Knights Templars bridged the River Thames that real prosperity came within the grasp of many. They wanted a link between Bisham Abbey and their chapel at Widmere.

The first wooden bridge in the twelfth century crossed from what is now the Compleat Angler Hotel in Berkshire to St Peter Street in Buckinghamshire, the latter then known as Duck Lane. That street name had nothing to do with swimming birds but was a reference to a ducking-stool on the riverbank! The lane served as Marlow's High Street for many years as a second bridge still linked the same points after the Civil War.

Soon after the construction of the original bridge the district boomed. The Manor of Merlaw became a focal point for markets and was renamed Chipping-Marlow soon after the opening of the new route, the word 'Chipping' indicating that markets were held there.

The Thames has been at the heart of almost everything affecting Marlow down the centuries. It supplied power for many mills and provided a good living for eel-catchers. Hundreds of barges used to ply the river. They played an important part in the life of Marlow, carrying away the products of the mills as well as timber and grain to London and for export. Raw materials for industry were unloaded at the wharves of Port Marlow.

On dry land there was a lot of horse-drawn transportation as well as pack mules and donkeys. When the Great Marlow Railway Company arrived in 1872 the 'iron horse' was dubbed 'The Marlow Donkey' and the name sticks to this day. The one and only passenger carriage was fitted with duplicated controls. On reaching Bourne End the driver could operate the train for the return journey from the rear of the coach instead of the footplate.

Before the arrival of the railway, Marlow provided many road services with stagecoaches and wagons. In the eighteenth and nineteenth centuries, based at the Crown Inn in High Street (where Lloyds Bank stands today and nothing to do with the Crown Hotel in Market Square of later years), the Marlow Flier went off twice a day to Piccadilly in London, a trip lasting three hours. There was also a wagon service twice a week from The Horns in Chapel Street to the New Inn by the Old Bailey in London, returning two days later.

As far back as the mid-1720s there was plenty of activity. Daniel Defoe visited the area and was obviously greatly impressed by all he saw. 'Marlow is a town of great embarkation on the Thames,' he wrote, 'not so much for goods wrought here (for the trade of the town is chiefly of bone lace) but for the goods from the neighbouring towns, and particularly a very great quantity of malt and meal is brought hither from High Wickham [Wycombe].'

He went on to describe in great detail the arrival at Marlow of malt, meal, paper and beech wood from the Buckinghamshire side of the river as well as all kinds of brasswork from Temple Mills, all transported away on barges.

Brewing and breweries have figured prominently in Marlow's history. There is a speculation that apart from the Wethered family, whose enterprise began officially in 1758, there were other breweries in the town. A nineteenth-century document describes Wethered's as 'the chief Brewery in Marlow'. The locations of the early breweries are unclear though it is believed the original premises were on the east side of High Street, in property demolished in 1960 because it was unsafe.

The great brewery empire was built up over more than two centuries to finish in its now-defunct site off High Street. During its existence Marlow Brewery carved out a name of consequence for the town under the Wethered family banner. It was by far the biggest employer of local labour and its products were distributed far and wide. Whitbread's took over in the 1980s and it was closed in 1992.

Industry still exists today but it is a very different kind of work, principally related to the electronic age and computer chip. Factories and plants have sprung up on land reclaimed from gravel pits off Fieldhouse Lane and now make a valuable contribution to employment.

Marlow's natural beauty has proved a magnet to thousands of people down the years. Artists, photographers, anglers, all kinds of boaters, sportsmen, as well as tourists and ramblers flock to the area every year. It has not all been cosmetic, however. Marlow Football Club was among the first fifteen clubs to subscribe to the original FA Cup. They reached the semifinal in 1881–2 and were semifinalists in the Amateur Cup twice. Marlow was the scourge of Berks and Bucks, winning the two counties trophy fourteen times.

On the Thames, Marlow Rowing Club has brought international fame to the town. Few people in the country have not heard of Steve Redgrave, the four times Olympic gold medallist who is now seeking a fifth in three years' time. He learned his skills with the Great Marlow School rowing four and Marlow Rowing Club before becoming a Leander member. In 1958 Geoffrey Baker from Cookham Dean and Michael Spracklen from Marlow won gold for rowing in the Commonwealth Games at Lake Padarn in North Wales.

Marlow Regatta – a separately constituted body with no administrative connection to Marlow Rowing Club – has grown into the largest one-day event of its kind in the world and certainly puts all other Thames regattas in the shade.

After the Second World War Marlow suffered the same fate as many other small towns and villages within a 50-mile radius of Charing Cross. People not only came to see the town . . . they wanted to live in it too.

So began a massive explosion of construction, swamping the 1,646 acres of the Urban District with new streets, houses and buildings. Within two decades the character of the quiet riverside beauty spot that had survived for many years as a Thames backwater was obliterated. But in spite of what has been done over the past forty years Marlow's most endearing features still remain prominent.

The suspension bridge over Old Father Thames, the spire of the parish church, the Compleat Angler Hotel, Marlow Weir downstream and the world-famous Regatta Reach above the bridge all combine to earn Marlow its unofficial, though richly deserved, title, 'The Jewel of the Thames'.

When extensive repairs were carried out on the steeple of the parish church in 1926, amateur photographers queued up to scale the scaffolding-clad spire. This view of Marlow Road, Bisham, on the Berkshire side of the Thames, shows the almost derelict appearance of the area around Marlow Rowing Club.

THAMES-SIDE

The highlight of each year in Marlow is the amateur regatta. The event is mainly organized by an independent committee but a lot of support is given by Marlow Rowing Club. This scene was typical of many in the Edwardian era when steam launches, punts and rowing-boats were used by the spectators.

These two aerial views of Marlow are separated by forty-six years. The picture above was captured by an Aerofilms-converted First World War bomber in June 1920. Below, from almost the same angle, is the 1966 version. It is obvious how development mushroomed in the intervening period – much of it in the years immediately after the Second World War. The bypass had yet to come to the east of the town, as had the intensive development of both industry and housing in the next thirty-one years.

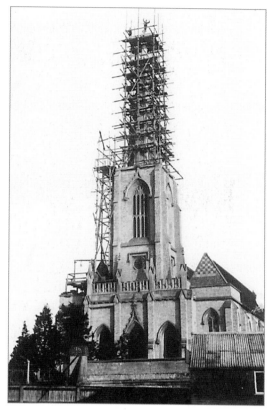

A gale damaged the spire of All Saints' Parish Church in 1899. It soon became a Mecca for the town's daredevils and photographers after scaffolding was erected to facilitate the repair. Percy Lovell, son of Young James Lovell the noted Marlow builder, celebrated part of his twenty-first birthday on 8 December of that year by scaling the metalwork and doing a jig. A number of other local worthies and characters, including furnishing shop proprietor from Market Square, Rupert Batting, also made the trip up the spire.

While these workmen who were carrying out the repairs were having their lunch at the Two Brewers in St Peter Street, an eleven-year-old girl also made the perilous trip to the top. She climbed down unaided to be greeted by the workmen, not with reprimand, but, so the story goes, with a watch to recognize her bravery.

Downstream from Marlow Bridge towards the weir stands the Compleat Angler Hotel, at one time considered to be part of Marlow itself. It is now in Berkshire. Where launches used to tie up at the frontage of the hotel, today helicopters land in the grounds at the rear as passengers bound for Ascot or other social events call in for coffee!

For more than 150 years All Saints' Parish Church spire has dominated the river scene. It is the third church on the site. The suspension bridge was built between 1829 and 1832, replacing two previous wooden structures downstream. The builder, William Tierney Clark, later used the project as a model to link Buda to Pest in Hungary by two similar, though much larger, structures.

A similar view of Marlow taken from the forecourt of the Compleat Angler Hotel in about 1900 clearly shows Shaw's Boathouse just upstream from the bridge. Punts, skiffs, and canoes could be hired from there. It was replaced by the Victorian Boathouse which was pulled down in the 1980s to make way for Tierney Court.

Marlow Lock has a chequered history as it replaced the 'death trap' system of rollers and cables that led to the demise of many bargees and river navigators. The pound lock proved to be a satisfactory alternative to mill-owners and river-users alike. The present lock-keeper's house is the third in the area though not built on the same site. Almost no commercial traffic uses the Thames today.

A much earlier view of Marlow Lock depicts the lock-keeper's cottage on its original site. The lock gates were manually operated and, in addition to allowing small boats to pass up or down the river, large vessels carrying passengers could also be accommodated.

The lock viewed from opposite the lock-keeper's cottage clearly shows the large beams used to open and close the gates as well as the wheels that operated the sluices to control water levels. The large white building in the distance on the left is Thames Lawn, once home to property millionaire Jack Cotton. Originally called Thames Bank it was occupied in the early nineteenth century by Vice-Admiral James Nicoll Morris who fought at Trafalgar with Nelson, commanding HMS *Colossus*.

Marlow weir is a spectacular sweep of tumbling water that stretches from just below the Compleat Angler Hotel to the entrance to Marlow Lock. In summer it gives a lot of pleasure to the eye; in winter it gives a lot of comfort to residents near the Thames as it plays a vital part in controlling the flow of water and preventing flooding. The lock-keeper, in constant touch by telephone to the nerve centre at Reading when danger threatens, has to operate the sluices above the weir from the catwalk visible on the left of the picture.

The cut into the lock is to the east of the weir. River-users tie up to wait their turn to enter the lock as it clears of upstream traffic. Old Bridge House, seen to the right of the church, was built at the bottom of St Peter Street and on the site of many cottages occupied by workers who had employment as coal porters, wharfmen and labourers at the breweries and mills. The tow-path began to disappear shortly after that time.

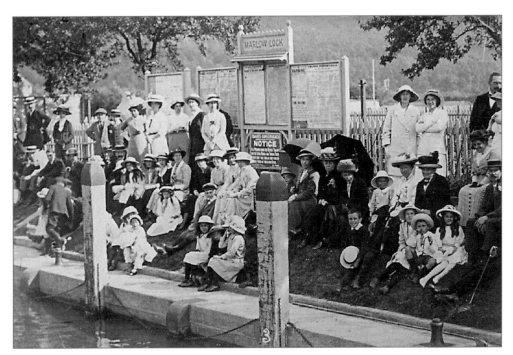

In the days before the steamer landing-stage in Higginson Park was built the place of embarkation was Marlow Lock. In 1910 this happy group of Sunday school children with their teachers and parents wait patiently for the steamer to take them on their annual picnic and trip upstream to Henley and back.

In the 1930s the number of pleasure craft on the river was increasing all the time. The era of the cabin cruiser was ushered in as more and more people took to the water for holidays and leisure. This 1932 commercial postcard illustrates the variety of motorized craft that became popular.

This family group pictured in about 1911–12 show there is nothing new in the pleasure of messing about on the river. The tow-path was still well defined and the reeds lasted many years before they were replaced with the present-day sandbag and concrete edging.

Thoughts of the balmy days of summer were very far from the minds of the Towers family and their friends when the Thames was frozen over in 1903. At the height of one of the most severe winters on record they trooped out on to the ice, not in the least fearful, and took the youngest member of the family with them in his pram. Posing for this remarkable photograph they picked the almost identical spot where Marlow Regatta races finished – just a few yards upstream from Marlow Rowing Club HQ.

Abject misery would affect many of Marlow's workforce in the depths of winter when the Thames used to rise well above normal levels and flood ground-floor living rooms and cellars. St Peter Street was particularly susceptible to this unwelcome intrusion.

This street was surprisingly not called Station Road until the railway arrived. Before that, it was most aptly dubbed Brook Street. While fewer properties were affected by the flooding than round the corner in St Peter Street, there was still cause for concern for many owners. Complaints made to authorities did not get much sympathy, as the gist of their replies was, 'People who live in riverside towns will get their feet wet sometimes'.

In the 1960s Marlow Urban Council agreed to plans for the Alder Meadows to be developed. This meant that Pound Lane, which had been a cul-de-sac as far as Court Garden Lodge for centuries, was opened up by a new road that ran all the way to Henley Road. Thus the way was opened for vast new housing estates. But before it was finally tamed the Thames had several flings and made its presence felt; numerous drivers found this out to their cost when they discovered their 'drowned engines'. It seemed appropriate that several closes were named after fish – Bream, Perch, Grayling, Trout, Marlin and Pike.

In South Place there was little to laugh about at certain times of the year. A retaining wall on the south side did little to deter the water and the residents had to resort to duckboards to get in and out of their street. As it was unlit there were also many problems at night.

Once a year the highly colourful 'Swan Uppers' travel up and down the Thames gathering and marking cygnets on behalf of Her Majesty the Queen, the Vintners and the Dyers livery companies. Captain John Turk, MVO (second from right), served as Her Majesty's Swan Keeper for thirty years, retiring in 1993. He took over in 1963 from his father who had held the position for forty-two years. Like his father before him, Captain Turk lives in Cookham where the family boat-hire business was based. Marlow is a very important area for the men who break their journeys and moor up their craft overnight before working up and downstream.

Marlow Rowing Club was founded in 1871. It owes much to Marlow Football Club which was formed the previous year under the direction of Colonel Tom Wethered. He inspired many local people to back the oarsmen and was president of both clubs at the same time. The original boathouse served the community well until 1971 – when it celebrated its 100th birthday. It was then agreed to extend the facilities by adding a second phase boathouse with new toilet block as well as a large social area.

SECTION TWO

THE TOWN

When the Lusitania was torpedoed by a German U-boat off the Irish coast in 1915 among those who perished was Charles Frohman. An American-born impresario, he staged many London West End shows. Frohman 'loved Marlow better than any place in the world' as he could relax away from the bright lights. His friends contributed to a memorial fund, the end product of which was this unique drinking fountain. Marlow's naked lady on The Causeway has been a talking point and target for vandals ever since.

Just how peaceful Marlow was in the early part of the twentieth century may be judged from this commercial postcard of The Causeway from about 1911. The state of the roads left much to be desired though the bulk of traffic in those days was horse drawn. Court Garden estate boundary was marked by a forbidding wall on the right, while Mr Carter's bakery and café continued in business until it was bought by Eric and Marie Burger in the early 1940s.

Once every year the Marlow men who gave their lives in the two world wars are remembered by a parade on Remembrance Sunday at The Causeway. The centre-piece of the Royal British Legion-sponsored ceremony is the town's war memorial which was unveiled on 26 July 1920. A wide cross-section of people take part in the service including town councillors, members of both adult and youth organizations, serving men and women from the Forces, including the United States Air Force and, most recently, the Maire and firemen from Marlow's twin town, Marly-le-Roi.

Wreaths are laid on the town's war memorial by all organizations attending the annual Remembrance Sunday parade in November 1964. Here Major Douglas Pluck, president of the Marlow branch of the Royal British Legion, begins the proceedings, watched by Revd Fred Horrox, minister of Marlow Congregational Church (later United Reformed Church), while High Wycombe Salvation Army band plays.

The strong youth representation was evident when Don Philpott, Commanding Officer of the Air Training Corps Squadron no. 1811, laid their wreath. The Guard of Honour was mounted by members of Marlow Sea Cadet Corps, from the training ship *Snipe* (later *Apollo*).

The names of all Marlow servicemen who fell in the First World War are not recorded on the town war memorial, but on a special tablet in All Saints' Parish Church.

The strong Georgian influence in Marlow High Street architecture is apparent in this view taken in 1909. Seen from The Causeway facing north, many of the buildings on the right were later swept away owing to neglect. The four cottages were part of a brewery at one time then later became shops and an optician's. A large building with car showrooms, owned by Currall Garages, was established beyond them.

Just how ruthless the developers were with the street scene is well illustrated by this view taken from almost the same vantage point in 1960. Properties on the west side of High Street, however, were hardly affected.

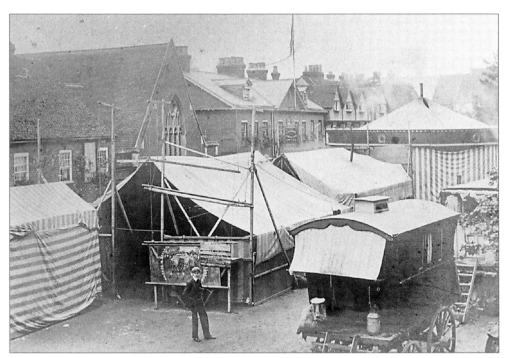

Any peace and tranquillity at The Causeway was shattered when Marlow Fair opened up in June. A hangover from the old days when farm labourers and mill-workers put themselves up for hire, the event caused a lot of resentment locally. It had lost its commercial value and become a nuisance – especially at night after the pubs closed!

It was not only The Causeway that suffered and caused complaints. The entire High Street, Market Square and the Common Slough (Spittal Square) became parking places for caravans as well as booths and stalls.

For much of the year there was little to get excited about in the High Street as this old postcard shows. What a contrast to the present-day hustle, bustle and vehicle congestion which occurs almost every working hour!

This commercial postcard on sale before the First World War almost leads one to believe Marlow was a 'one-horse' town. Nothing was further from the truth as the town heaved with hauliers and carriers.

Very little changed in Marlow's main street in the years immediately leading up to the First World War. This view taken in the mid-afternoon of 1912 emphasizes the interesting skyline on the east side of High Street.

Another pre-1914 view depicts the entrance to New Court on the right with the Crown Hotel dominating the town centre in Market Square. The modern resident and visitor must be impressed by the lack of vehicle traffic.

The building on the left of this 1906 photograph was the 1886 addition to the Crown Hotel. It replaced the former town hall, fire station and lock-up and continued trading successfully as an hotel until the early 1930s.

Although styling itself the Crown Hotel for many years after the Second World War, it was actually no longer residential. In what used to be the original hotel, shown on the right of this picture, the High Wycombe-based fruit and vegetable firm of H. & J.W. Aldridge traded in the smaller half of the ground floor with F.W. Woolworth as their neighbour. A hairdresser occupied the first floor and two residential flats were on the second.

What began as a hardware shop trading as Chalk and Newman was expanded by successive proprietors into a business that stocked many other lines including garden equipment and seeds, fishing tackle, boating gear and guns. The shop was held in high regard by people from a wide area and they were saddened when Cyril Chalk called it a day in 1990.

Such a prime site could not be left vacant for long, however. The new occupiers, travel agents Thomas Cook, have retained the original frontage.

Believed to be one of the oldest family butchers in the country, W.R. Clark was established in Marlow High Street in 1662. It traded continuously under various proprietors until 1996 when the management regretfully closed down because of the BSE scares sweeping the nation.

The premises have now been gutted though the façade has been preserved. Plans are going ahead to convert the building into a restaurant.

On the west side of the junction of High Street and Market Square stood Marlow's own department store. Morgan's was probably the biggest retail outlet in the town when this picture was taken in 1910. Between the two world wars the store was replaced by McIlroy's. In turn they were taken over by W.J. Daniel of Windsor who left the town in the early 1970s.

The frontage of the old department store has been radically amended by successive owners who operated several offices, including an estate agents and a bank.

The motor car began to make its presence felt in increasing numbers in Marlow soon after the end of the First World War. But one man who preferred his pedal tricycle was a local doctor, seen here in 1921, carrying his little black bag in a basket on the handlebars.

Very few large-scale retailers patronized Marlow before the Second World War. A noted exception was this branch of Freeman, Hardy & Willis, a national boot and shoe supplier, whose High Street premises were next to the arched entrance to New Court (on the left) seen here in 1890. In the early 1900s they crossed High Street and continued trading until the late 1950s.

A Princes Risborough family moved into Marlow in 1855 and opened up a grocer's business in West Street. Soon after the shop was moved to Spittal Street. The double-fronted shop, pictured here in 1880, later became a greengrocer's with a watch and clock repair and sales shop next door. G. Dorsett & Son had moved again, this time to Market Square.

A hundred years after the firm was founded, George Dorsett, nephew of the founder, and his wife Nellie drink to the success of the business in Market Square in 1955. But sad to tell, supermarkets and an out-of-town superstore put an end to the enterprise and it folded in 1965.

Barnard, Son & Company operated a general goods and tobacco store in Spittal Street for many years after the First World War. In the centre of this picture is the Greyhound Hotel while on the left, jutting out into the Common Slough (Spittal Square), is the half-timbered gable end of the Odeon cinema. The buildings between are on the east side of Dean Street and have long since been demolished, the sites now providing space for two car parks and Marlow's open-air market on Wednesdays and Saturdays.

Mr and Mrs L.E. Robinson operated their hardware and ironmongery business from the Barnard's provisions shop premises for many years, and with considerable success. When they retired in 1989 workmen arrived to establish two small shops within the double-fronted area. As they removed the Robinson fascia they uncovered the original and very well-preserved Barnard sign.

Many little shops were a feature of Spittal Street between the wars; offices came more recently. This little family business was a great favourite of children as there was always a wide variety of confectionery for sale. On the east side stood the Odeon or 'picture palace' as Marlow folk called it. It closed in the early 1930s when a grand new cinema was opened in Station Road. But the building was in use in the 1960s and early 1970s as a factory turning out millions of 'Poppet' plastic interlocking beads.

The old cinema and several shops were demolished to make way for this multiple suite of offices, originally known as Maritz House. That company has now relocated to Globe Park trading estate and the Spittal Square offices have been renamed Windsor House.

For many years before the Second World War, Sid Harris of Frieth Road operated the saddler's and leather goods business of John Harleigh in Spittal Street. He did business with many farmers who worked with horses and also repaired their machine canvas. This was how the shop looked in 1947 when the current proprietor, Ken Drucquer, bought it.

In 1964 Mr Drucquer had the frontage remodelled. In addition to the range of products sold he incorporated a wide range of sports equipment. He was for many years secretary of both Marlow Sports Club in Pound Lane and Marlow Cricket Club.

In an agricultural area such as Marlow there was great opportunity for feed, corn and seed merchants. One of the more successful firms was run by the Webb family, pictured here outside their Dean Street premises. The double doors on the right led to their spacious yard where grain and fertilisers were stored.

A great many pubs in Dean Street led to the area being dubbed 'The City' by Marlow wags. Three pubs – the Bank of England to the north, the Royal Exchange halfway down and The Mint near Spittal Street junction – gave rise to this. Another popular Dean Street house was the Cherry Tree, pictured here in 1912. The lady licensee, Mrs Clark, is standing at the door. On the other side of the street was Harvey's the baker's. Mr Harvey and son are standing outside the green-tiled façade. The man with the child was the local chimney-sweep who lived in property at the rear of the pub.

The Cherry Tree was shut by Wethered's in 1935. It was used as a dairy by twin brothers Bob and Harry Hughes for years after that. Demolished completely in 1996, the old pub, as well as a shoe-repair business, made way for this modern shop and office development. The only link with the past is that the new enterprise has been called Cherry Tree House.

It was an odd coincidence in 1903 when the showmen visiting the town with Marlow Fair chose to set up their mobile 'picture palace' outside the area where the Odeon was eventually established. On the right stood the original Cross Keys pub. Revised building lines demanded it be demolished in 1912 and rebuilt several yards back from the road.

More planning mayhem hit the site next door to the Cross Keys in the 1960s after the Boddy family left the newsagent's on the right. Bill Bunce's fish and chip shop and George Aughton's greengrocer's stood for only six years then they all came down. A parade including a launderette, a branch of Tesco, a frozen food shop and a draper's was rebuilt. In less than twenty years they too were demolished. Now Angler's Court has replaced everything.

Chapel Street still carries the main road out of town to High Wycombe and Bourne End. The Barnard family had a branch in this street as well as Spittal Street. By the lamppost on the right is a low railing that was the entrance to a mid-nineteenth-century chapel – today Marlow Community HQ at Liston Hall. It is unlikely the street was named after this chapel. The railings and houses have gone to create the main entrance to a large car park and offices have replaced the bakery with the sun-blind.

In the 1930s there were two Marlow sub-post offices, one in Dean Street and this one in Wycombe Road. Miss Alice Truss, standing on the doorstep, ran it for many years with her relatives. As well as the post office counter service the shop sold a wide range of other goods. In summer, teas were served in the garden and when Marlow Football Club had a home match round the corner in Oak Tree Road, cycles and cars were parked outside.

Marlow had more than its fair share of the poor and needy in days gone by. In 1608 a Catholic recusant and owner of Marlow Mill founded a charity for poor parishioners. His almshouses in Oxford Lane (as it was known then) lasted well until 1968 when it was decided to demolish and rebuild on the same site. The bulldozers did not take long to remove the Brinkhurst bequest, which was funded originally by wharf tolls on Marlow's river frontage.

West Street carries the A4155 to Henley and, despite the bypass relieving a lot of traffic, this is still one of the busiest thoroughfares in Marlow. It leads to the central car park off Oxford Road, patronized by hundreds of shoppers every day. Farther on is Chalk Pit Lane leading to many villages and the Chilterns. When this postcard was produced there was little evidence of what was to come later in the twentieth century.

Varied developments down the years have resulted in this very interesting West Street skyline that remains to the present day. On the left, the White Lion pub is now a local garage firm's showrooms; opposite, the Red Lion still exists, but the cottages on the right of the picture have gone to make way for a car park.

This early 1900s postcard gives an air of wealth and activity to West Street. The feeling was not misplaced, for many rich and famous people made their homes there. Horses and carts are much in evidence as well as a solo horseman.

Station Road was renamed soon after the introduction of the railway service from Bourne End by the Marlow Railway Company in 1872. The first trains did not arrive until the following year but after that many feet beat a path to sample this new mode of transport. They still do every working day.

Very little had changed in Station Road by the 1960s. Electric lamps replaced the old gas standards for street lighting. Some shops had changed hands or been improved. The Wheatsheaf pub was closed for the last time though its memory is preserved on the ground-glass panel of what is now the front door of a private house, proclaiming 'Jug & Bottle Entrance'.

Probably the best surviving example of fourteenth-century domestic architecture in Buckinghamshire, the Old Parsonage still proudly stands at the junction of St Peter Street and Station Road. At one stage in its history it provided accommodation for the clergy, as the name implies, but for much of the nineteenth century to the present day it has been occupied by laypeople.

A picture of St Peter Street in 1910 shows the girls' school on the left. The building with the circular window was the public hall and is now the Masonic Centre. In the background, but dominating the area, is Marlow Place in Station Road, while to the right are the Old Parsonage and The Presbytery.

One of Marlow's best respected shopkeepers, Miss Cissie ('Cis') Davis, inherited the newsagent's business, Geo. Davis, from her father and ran it until the 1980s. In addition to early starts in the morning to sort out the newspapers, Cis also handled the confectionery and tobacco side of the business at 7 Spittal Street with some part-time help. She died in October 1983 aged seventy-eight years.

Before Phil and Audrey Dorsett left Marlow in 1965, after winding up their 110-year-old grocery business in Market Square, they celebrated their Silver Wedding by remarrying in the parish church. They went to live at West Moors in Dorset, where Phil managed various supermarkets in Wimborne and Tucton. A talented organist and musician, he formed the West Moors Singers for which he is still annually remembered. His widow continues to reside in West Moors.

LOCAL GOVERNMENT

In 1974 Marlow Urban Council went out of existence after seventy-eight years of managing the 1,646 acres that was Marlow. It was replaced by Wycombe District Council. However, a successor town council was permitted under the new legislation headed by a town mayor. When the town mayor, Miss Diana McColl, did the rounds of other local authorities she noticed that they all had splendid badges of office. Her enquiries revealed that the badge on Marlow's chain of office was not recognized officially. So began a campaign to have official armorial bearings. The town council agreed to this but found the cost prohibitive for such a small authority. Then a former town mayor, Mr Francis Murray, backed by his sister and brothers, agreed to meet the bill in memory of their late father who had died only a few months previously.

Sir William Borlase's School in West Street was founded in 1624 to teach twenty-four boys to read, write and count. Nearby was another building for twenty-four girls to be taught lace-making. It became a boys' grammar school in 1881 and was a male preserve until 1988, when girls were admitted. For some years there was a boarding house at Sentry Hill off Henley Road but this was sold off in the late 1980s.

As Marlow's population increased and the town expanded in the west a new school became vital. Spinfield County Combined School was opened in the late 1970s. Their annual fête in the spacious grounds attracted many well-known personalities. Author Roald Dahl opened the 1987 event, using the occasion to plug his new book *James and the Giant Peach*.

The privately run Dial Close School was opened at The Causeway by Mrs Gerrans in 1929. During its existence it attracted the children of many local well-to-do parents from farms around the town as well as business people.

Dial Close School was overtaken by economics and closed in 1972. The final speech day took place in the main hall of Borlase School when the prizes were presented by a former pupil, Mr Alan Coster.

A Roman Catholic school was opened in St Peter Street, adjacent to the church, in 1845. Increased population demands were met in the early 1980s by moving to Prospect Road. It was a great day for the children when headmaster Mr Bob Pyle took delivery of this minibus, a gift from the parents' association.

Sports always featured strongly at Borlase School. The rugger XV of 1936 was unbeaten. The squad shown is, back row, left to right: Laidlaw, Martin, -?-, Wethered, geography master, Mr Kent from New Zealand, -?-, -?-, Clarke. Front row: Highley, Boyce, Ostroumoff, Salter, Percy Collins, -?-, -?-. Seated are Peter Lloyd and ? Sendall.

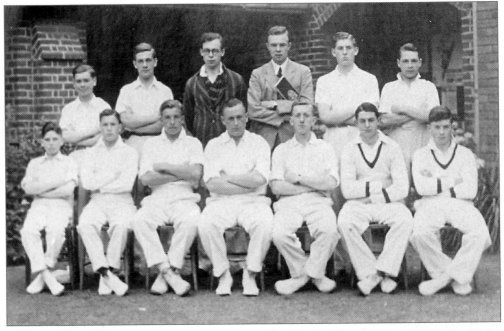

The cricket XI of 1939. Back row, left to right: Belsham, Clarke, Mr Kent, -?-, Highley and Peter Lloyd. Front row: Ken Palmer, -?-, Dennis Tew (destined to be physical training master at Great Marlow School in the 1960s), Ostroumoff, Stone, Laidlaw and Malyon.

Great Marlow School was opened in September 1961. The move took a lot of strain off Holy Trinity C of E School in Wethered Road. Great Marlow PTA ran many successful fêtes to bolster school funds. Bisham resident Patricia (Paddy) Green who plays Jill in *The Archers* (second from left) opened proceedings in 1974, accompanied by the PTA chairman, Mrs Dick Price. The school's most famous product to date is Steve Redgrave, four times Olympic gold medallist.

There were many well-loved teachers on the staff of Holy Trinity C of E Middle School over the years, none more than Miss Daphne Drew, seen here on her retirement day in the main hall in 1985.

These were the dresses worn by the schoolgirls who attended Marlow Girls' School in St Peter Street in 1896. Many of them came from poor families so there was never any question of a school uniform being introduced. Until it closed down in 1960 (it opened in 1871), the school was served by a succession of dedicated teachers.

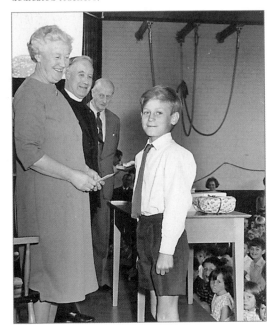

The last headmistress of Marlow Girls' School, Miss Christine Webber from Luton, was appointed in about 1946/7. When it closed in 1960, Miss Webber went to Holy Trinity C of E School in Wethered Road. On her retirement many gifts were presented, this one from the boys in the school. The vicar of Marlow, Canon Dr Sam Day, and Commander Owen Wethered, a school governor, look on.

The official opening of the new school quarters took place in 1956 when Lady Pretty, wife of the CO of no. 90 Group, and Marlow garage proprietor, County Councillor George Currall of Bucks Education Committee, did the honours.

Danesfield School began with primary status in 1955. It was a collection of huts at Rassler Wood, Medmenham, which catered for families of RAF personnel at Signals Command HQ as well as eligible local children. The first headmistress there, Miss Gladys Belson, retired in 1972.

This was the last meeting of Marlow Urban Council in 1974; Cyril Chalk presided. The four council members on the left were Aubrey Maynard, Robert Fyfe, Maurice Oram and Daphne Jones. David Rogers (surveyor) is sitting in front of Harry Howe, housing manager and Tom Jackson, clerk/engineer. Brooke Furmston (vice chairman) is on the chairman's left with Miss Dorothy Sendall, finance officer, seated in front of Mrs Dorothy Barton (administration). The three remaining councillors are John Hester, Bill Tillier and Frank Edmonds with Jack Burslem (public health) seated on the extreme right.

Democracy at work! In 1972 residents of River Park Drive and Hyde Green objected to a timber yard on the site of the old railway station – especially the running of a cyclone dust extractor. Some wag conned a hearing-aid company salesman into seeing Tom Jackson, Marlow Council clerk and engineer! But this massive petition did much more good in the end as it led to the formation of the Marlow Residents' Association. John Carvell (smoking the pipe) and Leslie Wells (fourth from the right) became elected council members.

As a fighter pilot in the First World War defending Edinburgh from Zeppelins, Aubrey Ward from East Anglia was stationed at East Fortune aerodrome. In Berwick-upon-Tweed he met Miss Rutherford, daughter of a West Street draper, and they married. In civil life he was a veterinary surgeon, practising in Slough where he became mayor. He was elected to Buckinghamshire County Council and served a term as chairman for which he was knighted in 1971. He and Lady Ward retired to Marlow where they celebrated both golden and diamond weddings. Now a residential home for the elderly in Prospect Road, Marlow, bears his name.

Lawyer John Routly of Woodend House, Marlow, was a Bucks County Council member for fifteen years from 1965 and a past chairman. He and his wife Joan, a former magistrate on the Marlow bench, went to live in Shrewsbury when he retired so as to be within easy reach of the Blaenau Ffestiniog Railway of which he was chairman for some time.

This was the unofficial emblem that served many Marlow clubs and organizations until the adoption of the present coat of arms.

Increasing pressure for building land in 1967 made Marlow Urban Council think about high-rise development. Hanging Hill was a possible site. Bucks County Council planning staff floated this red balloon 200 ft above the area to give some idea of what would be involved.

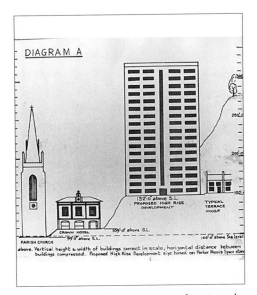

Marlow Society, however, warned against the project. Artist David Gerrans drew this impression of what the building would look like. The scheme never happened and consequently a four-storey limit was placed on all future buildings.

Marlow town band owes its origins to the Church Lads' drum and fife band of the nineteenth century. In 1906 the brass band was formed by John Palmer from Chesham who set up business as a shoemaker in Station Road. The original band hall was built by the bandsmen in 1937/8 from a store donated by Benny Picton of High Wycombe. Marlow Sea Cadet Corps were founded in the band hall in the 1960s. Eventually a brick-built two-storey HQ was built on the site in the late 1970s. The band use the hall twice a week for practice. Brian Palmer (on the right in the picture), grandson of the founder, has given up conducting and is now president.

CLUBS & SERVICES

General Sir George Higginson GCV GCVO, must rank as one of Marlow's most prominent citizens. He lived at Gyldernscroft in Henley Road. He is best remembered for his patronage of the fund that led to Higginson Park becoming one of Marlow's greatest public assets. Court Garden house and grounds went on the market in 1920 when Mr Robert Griffin died. It was rumoured that the estate was to be broken up and individual villas built: this appalled the town. Canon M. Graves, Mr L.J. Smith and Mr R.H. Cathcart began raising funds to buy the house and surrounding land. They succeeded and on his 100th birthday on 5 July 1926, Sir George was presented with the keys to the park while his old regimental band, the Grenadier Guards, played 'Happy Birthday to you'. In the presence of Princess Mary, the Princess Royal, he handed the keys back to Marlow. Sir George, a veteran of the Crimean War and at one time aide-de-camp to Queen Victoria, had many other local strings to his bow. He was chairman of Marlow magistrates for a time; he founded Bovingdon Green School in Spinfield Lane; he also helped in the founding of Marlow Cottage Hospital and opened it on 4 August 1915.

Sir William Clayton of Harleyford Manor was responsible for the formation of the Royal Bucks Yeomanry in 1834. They eventually became the Royal Bucks Hussars. Sir William's family could trace its origins back to the arrival of William the Conqueror. One of his ancestors, Roger de Claytone, was William's personal standard bearer, so there was always a military background to the family. Another member of the Claytons fought in the Peninsula War and at Waterloo his great black charger, Skirmisher, was fatally wounded in the advance on Paris. It was buried in Colonel's Meadow at Borlase School. A tablet in the grounds of Harleyford Manor commemorates both the horse and its owner's exploits.

A troop train brought these men to Marlow Station in 1915. They marched to Marlow Common and Bovingdon Green where various billets were provided, as well as at Spinfield. The object of their presence was to train them for the digging and fitting out of trenches in the conflict overseas in France and elsewhere. The practice earthworks remain to this day. Known locally as 'The Trenches', they are inhabited by many adders each summer.

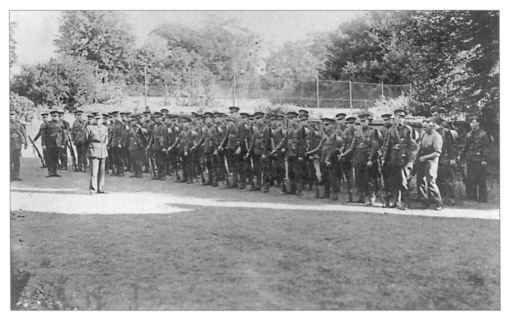

Getting ready for an inspection prior to leaving the Marlow area in 1915. These troops were among the many who were trained in the art of digging trenches on Marlow Common.

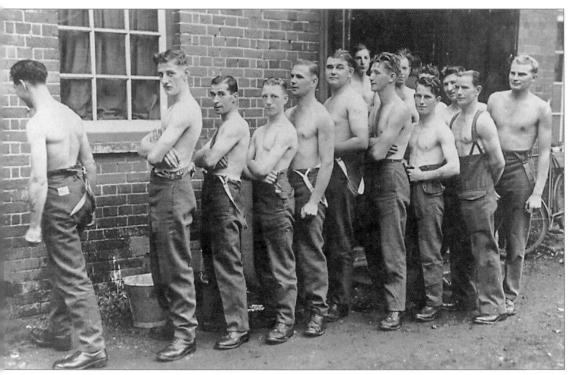

With war threatening in 1938 these Buckinghamshire lads volunteered for and joined the 2nd Battalion, Ox and Bucks Light Infantry (TA). They were quickly lined up outside The Armoury and Drill Hall in Institute Road, Marlow, for their medicals.

Not long after becoming 'Terriers' in the Territorial Army in 1938, this group of Bucks lads was soon in uniform. On Saturday 2 September 1939, they were all mobilized and assembled at The Armoury in Marlow, ready for the conflict that broke out next morning.

After their march to Wooburn the Terriers were joined with this group of men who comprised A Company, 1st Battalion of the Buckinghamshire Light Infantry (TA). The 1st Battalion went to France in 1940 and of the 1,001 men who served there, fewer than 200 returned. As a result the battalion was disbanded.

Edward ('Ted') Sturt was born at Fenny Stratford, Bucks, in 1894. He joined Buckinghamshire Constabulary when he was eighteen. After service with the Royal Garrison Artillery in Belgium in the First World War he returned to policing. Promoted to Divisional Inspector in charge of South-West Division, Marlow, he retired in 1949 after thirty-three years service. He received the King's Police Medal during this time.

Chief Inspector Bernard Loosley DFM, was an air gunner in Lancaster bombers during the Second World War. He joined Bucks Constabulary after the war and, following several promotions, took charge at Marlow in 1957 until he retired. He represented Thames Valley Police in Marly-le-Roi, near Paris, at the Jumelage celebrations in 1973. He is seen here in front of the French national police band.

Shortly before the Second World War broke out there was a rally of all Marlow-section Bucks Special Constabulary at Court Garden. Here the first of many training sessions to deal with anticipated emergencies took place.

Dorothy Earl (left) was Marlow's first active policewoman in the early 1950s. She is pictured here with her husband George Earl (right) who, in partnership with Bill Green, ran a garage business in Little Marlow Road for many years, up until the early 1980s.

Police Constable Cyril Claridge (centre) was a very long-serving member of Buckinghamshire Constabulary who continued his service with Thames Valley Police after the merging of forces. Much of his time was spent in Marlow and Bourne End. He is pictured in the Clayton Arms, Marlow, at his retirement party with his wife and Superintendent Ken Lovegrove.

Established at Foxes Piece allotments in 1938 the Royal Observer Corps post in Marlow attracted many businessmen during the Second World War. Ken Hadfield from Hurley, seen here between Chief Observer Officer Bourne (left) and Observer Officer Reid, was presented with his long service medal in The Chequers. Also pictured are Observer Merrick Brown and Chief Observer Ken Palmer (left), and Observer John Standstead (right).

Theo Lunnon DSM served with the motor torpedo boats during the Second World War. He helped found Marlow Sea Cadet Corps and was the second CO with the rank of lieutenant-commander. Parade marshal at several Remembrance Sunday services, he was also a sergeant with Marlow Special Constables and was foreman mechanic at Angus Wellicome's High Street garage.

Ron Anson (right) was also a founder of the training ship *Snipe* with Theo Lunnon. He served the unit as Chief Petty Officer and trained cadets to row and sail on the Thames. He was also a Marlow Special Constable.

Marlow's first fire-engine was a small hand-drawn affair, a gift to the town by one John Clavering in 1731. It was parked in the entrance to the parish church. By 1909 a much larger machine was on the scene. It was garaged in one of the arches in the town hall frontage in Market Square. The trouble was, when there was a fire these chaps had to catch the horses first.

Marlow town centre came to a grinding halt in 1920 when a large crowd gathered to see the arrival of the town's new petrol-driven fire-engine. The authorities planned a happy and colourful occasion but the weather put a damper on things.

This was what that crowd had been waiting for. 'Vera' – believed to have been named after Lady Terrington of Spinfield Park – was to prove a big improvement. The volunteer firemen represented many famous Marlow family names including Chalk, Sawyer, Bowles, Shaw and Price.

Councillor Cyril Chalk (fourth from left), who followed in his father's footsteps into the family High Street hardware business, did not take after his Dad so far as the fire service was concerned. Mr Chalk senior was fire chief in Marlow for many years. When Cyril paid a visit in 1973, as chairman of Marlow Urban Council, he must have realized then how much fun he had missed out on.

Marlow fire station personnel turned out in their Cambridge Road headquarters in 1960 to say farewell to Station Officer Gilbert Price (sixth from left in the centre row). Four of his future successors are in the group: Fred Simmons, Bob Howard, Geoffrey Illingworth and Mike Jackson.

Tom Jeskins (centre) became licensee of the Carpenter's Arms in Spittal Street in 1967. He moved there from The Globe in High Wycombe. That year he was in the chair of the Marlow branch of the RAOB (Buffaloes). At the most important meeting of the year for the branch Tom welcomed the national president, Bob Arnold (second from left), who played Tom Forrest in *The Archers* radio programme.

Marlow Cottage Hospital was originally set up in Cambridge Road in 1889. In 1915 the hospital was moved to the brand-new building off Glade Road and Victoria Road. General Sir George Higginson cut the ribbon; bookmaker Jack Langley was the inspiration behind the fund-raising. Now Marlow Community Hospital boasts many departments – much support coming from the League of Friends.

Little Frank Towers was just two when this snap was taken in Quoiting Square. The background shows Clark's butcher's shop (no relation to the High Street firm) with double doors leading to their own slaughterhouse. Frank became a surveyor and after retiring from the brewery spent much time planning and designing stages in the building of the Community Hospital.

Mrs Millie Hester was a volunteer nurse with the St John Ambulance Brigade in Marlow for many years. She received the national award of Serving Sister in 1989 for her caring work with the elderly. St John Ambulance was established in Marlow over 100 years ago.

The British Red Cross Society in Marlow longed to have their own place for many years. Finally, in April 1967, the great day arrived when the Duchess of Kent officially opened the custom-built centre at the rear of Marlow Hospital. Local architect Mr Courtenay Constantine was the designer. The Red Cross cadets were thrilled to meet the Royal visitor.

There has never been any shortage of volunteer helpers in the many Marlow medical establishments. Mrs Doris Waller received this gift of a coffee percolator and cups in recognition of her fifteen years service as secretary to the Baby Clinic. With her are (left to right) Miss Sylvia Turner (Health Visitor) and district nurses Dorothea Ruddick and Nan Hackett.

Funds are always welcomed to supplement those provided by the Trustees at Brinkhirst, the former almshouses off Oxford Road. Mrs Gwendoline Pounds MBE (left), town mayor and town council representative on the charity, led willing helpers every year. Today an old people's accommodation development off Sandygate Road bears her name in her memory – Gweneth Court. She had been known as Gweneth all the time she lived in Marlow.

Marlow Round Table was formed in the early 1960s. Wives of the Tablers established their opposite organization, the Ladies' Circle, soon after. Here they were celebrating their first ten years of existence at The Chequers.

There was no Rotary Club in Marly-le-Roi, Marlow's twin town outside Paris. So Marlow Rotarians did the next best thing and twinned with the neighbouring French town, La Celle St Cloud. In 1985 the French club visited Marlow and a reception was held at Sentry Hill, Borlase School boarding house, thanks to the headmaster, Rotarian Roy Smith.

Rotarian Don Sawyer was the twenty-fifth president of Marlow Rotary Club. He and his wife Marjorie, who jointly ran a funeral directors' business, cut the celebratory cake.

Vicar of Little Marlow, the Revd Alex Jayne (left), secretary of Marlow Rotary Club in the 1960s and 1970s, weighs up the quality of entries at the annual schools' art exhibition. This was staged by the club and held in Court Garden. With him is Ron Compton, one of the organizers.

Every summer crowds pour into Higginson Park on Saturdays when a succession of fêtes take place. These raise money to support local organizations and their charities. People in this typical crowd were watching a children's fancy-dress competition at Marlow Round Table fête in 1976.

A few years later the Tablers brought Chitty Chitty Bang Bang – the make-believe Ian Fleming car that starred in the film of the same name – to Higginson Park. There was more than a passing interest as a lot of the film was shot at Hambleden village and the Turville Valley just outside Marlow.

Marlow has never been slow to support charities at either local or national level. Tony Boddy (right), licensee of the Clayton Arms, Lane End, and chairman of Marlow LVA for four years in the 1980s, hands over a cheque to Eric Rance, representative of the Denham LV National Homes in February 1972. Mr Boddy and his wife Nina formerly ran a newsagent's business in Spittal Street, Marlow.

Chairwoman of Marlow Urban Council, councillor Mrs Ruth Jewell, scales a stepladder outside New Court in Marlow High Street to mark off the final donations to the Winston Churchill Memorial Fund in September 1969. A wide programme of events was organized to reach the total.

When All Saints' Parish Church needed funds to repair its unique Father Willis organ, members of the congregation set about raising the wind in fine style. Pirates of all shapes and sizes descended on the town one Saturday in 1955, made a good start for the organ fund and had a lot of fun at the same time.

Two shows are staged annually by Marlow Horticultural Society in the Shelley Theatre at Court Garden. Of the two, the summer event on August Bank Holiday Monday draws the biggest interest both in entries and from the public. Discerning eyes, however, do not always agree with the judges.

In the dying days of Marlow Urban Council in 1972 a lot of pressure was exerted by Marlow Community Association for the council to develop The Rookery as their headquarters and centre. The big house formerly occupied by Captain Wright and his family, but vacant since his death, was demolished. The Community Association even named the area 'Wrightlands' – but the development never happened and Marlow gained another park instead.

The association was then offered Liston Hall off Chapel Street for their centre and they grabbed the chance. Mrs Dorothy Bruce (right), wife of a local GP from Henley Road, was one of the main people to get the project up and running.

A whole range of groups sprouted up once the Community Association was fully established. Dog training was among the first of the classes offered and it figured weekly. There followed a host of activities for both old and young alike including the Cameo, Four Seasons and the Friday clubs, in addition to the Bridge Club and Scottish dancing.

Where are they now? These Marlow youngsters were full of beans and making the most of the facilities at the Mothers and Toddlers group in Liston Hall in about 1975.

Marlow just loves processions. This remarkable photograph taken at The Causeway in about 1900 may have been part of the town's celebrations of Queen Victoria's Diamond Jubilee.

No doubt, however, about why these decorations graced the High Street. They were produced by a dedicated group of workers, headed by architect Mr Courtenay Constantine of West Street, to celebrate the coronation of the Queen in 1953. Three coronets each weighing 2½ hundredweight were borne by poles bearing emblems of swans and suspended over the street. They were also illuminated at night. Marlow's decorations were the envy of all the neighbouring towns.

The High Street decorations for the coronation in 1937 were not quite so elaborate but the flags of all the nations in the Empire mingled with many Union Jacks and made a brave show.

Coronation Day on 12 May 1937, and almost every haulage firm in the area had their lorries pressed into service to mount tableaux. The streets were lined with cheering crowds as the procession toured the town.

The Maids of Honour.

Miss Evelyn Plumridge.   Miss Mary Penny.

Miss Gladys Clement.   (Portraits by Greville, Marlow).   Miss Millicent Dean.

In the run-up to the celebrations for the coronation of King George VI and Queen Elizabeth the town chose its own personalities to head local activities. Winner of the Marlow Coronation Carnival Queen competition was Miss Alice Frith. She was chosen by film star Mary Pickford and crowned by Lady Victor Paget.

The Coronation Carnival Queen was attended by four maids of honour: Miss Evelyn Plumridge, Miss Mary Penny, Miss Millicent Dean and Miss Gladys Clement.

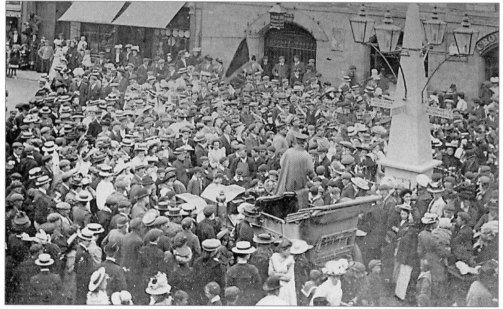

Another important occasion, when it seemed all Marlow turned out in Market Square, was the visit of General Booth, head of the Salvation Army, in 1911. Standing in the back of an open-topped car he addressed the people. This must have made a lasting impression, for the Citadel in Crown Road was established in 1931 and has had a large following in Marlow ever since.

The encouragement of youth has always been a strong policy of the Salvation Army in Marlow. These youngsters had just taken part in a Sunday concert in the Citadel in Crown Road. Captain Snell, the officer in charge at Marlow in those days, is on the left and his wife is on the right. The girls pictured (maiden names, of course) are, back row, left to right: Maureen Hook, Maureen West, Shirley Winterbourne and Sheila Bowles. Middle row: Pam Fletcher, Edith Winterbourne, Heather Savin, Marion Budd and Janet Hook. Front row: Kay West, Sylvia Bowles, Verena Barnes and Sandra Reece.

This photograph, also taken at the Crown Road Citadel in about 1940, depicts some real old Marlow characters. One of the best known was Granny Winterbourne, seated third from the left in the middle row. She never quibbled when she was called out, day or night, either to deliver babies or lay out the dead.

The Bishop of Buckingham, Rt Revd Christopher Pepys (left), conducted a confirmation service in Marlow Parish Church in 1970. He was assisted by the vicar of Marlow, Canon Dr Sam Day, who served Marlow for twenty-three years from 1966 until he retired in 1989. Bishop Pepys died in 1977.

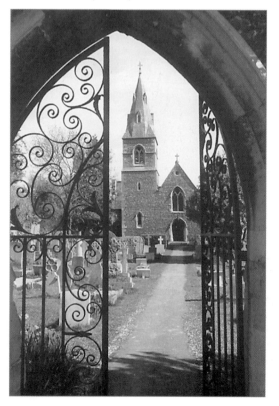

St Peter's Roman Catholic Church, designed by Pugin, was built in 1846 and a school was opened next door soon after. The grave of James L. Molloy, who composed the well-known ballad 'Love's Old Sweet Song', is marked by a Celtic cross in the churchyard. The school moved to Prospect Road in the 1980s.

From small beginnings the congregation of St Peter's outgrew the accommodation. In the mid-1960s it was decided to add to the building. The Bishop of Northampton dedicated the completed part of the church in 1971.

Painstaking work on the extension was carried out by Mr Jock Murray and his five sons. Great care was taken to make the new building blend with, and not detract from, the Pugin masterpiece.

One of the most colourful and humorous floats in the 1937 Coronation Carnival was the entry from Y.J. Lovell, the Marlow-based building firm. Members of staff from the High Street works became a menagerie for the day under the guidance of works' foreman Ted Sewell, looking out from the cab.

Tillion and Sons operated a large haulage business from the rear of The Horns pub in Chapel Street. Their lorries and drivers were in great demand on Coronation Day, to take part in the carnival procession.

COMMERCE & INDUSTRY

It used to be said in the depressed days between the wars that Marlow only had two industries – the making of beer . . . and the drinking of it! This was an oversimplification then and it is certainly far from the truth now. For centuries the water-powered Marlow Mills dominated the Bucks bank of the Thames turning out a wide variety of goods including meal, paper and flour. Probably the biggest employer of labour was the brewery owned by the Wethered family. Agriculture always played an important part in the life of the area and it still does to the present day, though it is nowhere near as labour-intensive as in past times.

It was not all brewing beer during the First World War at Wethered's. This group photograph of munitions workers who turned out mortar bombs and a variety of shells was taken at the brewery off High Street in 1915.

Horse-drawn drays were the lifeblood of Wethered's distribution business for years. At the turn of the century, however, they introduced steam-driven lorries, then followed a succession of petrol-driven trucks. One of these still survives to the present day. It makes frequent appearances at fêtes and shows or on 'special deliveries' when new brews come on the market.

Safe driving by their draymen was always emphasized and encouraged by Wethered's management. It was a particularly good year for the men from Marlow in 1920. This display of trophies and medals shows that they were very successful at several national and local competitions.

A new breed of draymen came on the scene after the end of the Second World War. In 1957 a brand-new fleet of lorries arrived at Marlow depot. The old horses were commemorated with brass plates bearing their names which were fixed to the new vehicles.

Although aesthetically pleasing to the eye, Marlow's famous suspension bridge has frequently caused a great deal of upset. Built in three years, between 1829 and 1832, the structure was intended for horses and carts only. By 1926 the road surface was in need of major surgery by these workmen. But there was little traffic to worry about in those days.

By 1964 the bridge was considered dangerous. A tank on a transporter, crossing in 1951, had not helped but when suspenders began to break in 1963 a major job was planned. Work went on twenty-four hours a day, seven days a week. When completed the bridge looked the same but modern materials were expected to extend its life for many years.

Ingenious planning meant vehicles under 2 tons could use a catwalk built over the bridge surface. One-way traffic flow was controlled by traffic lights. This view shows cars coming from Bisham in 1965.

Traffic leaving Marlow often queued as far back as High Street. The most famous 'customers' were the Great Train Robbers on their way from Durham Jail to the Isle of Wight in a spectacular police convoy.

Local opinions prevailed in the end as Marlow Bridge was retained and the Marlow–Bisham bypass was built. The main element on the new road is Thames Bridge, well downstream from the town.

It was a great day for Marlow on 20 December 1972 when the new bypass was officially opened. Doing the honours in unison were the Lord Lieutenants of both Buckinghamshire and the Royal County of Berkshire. The Lord Lieutenant of Buckinghamshire, Major John Darling Young, JP, is on the left. The Hon. David John Smith is on the right.

Watching with considerable satisfaction were some of the men who helped in the construction of the £4¼ million project.

When the bypass was built the public footpath connecting the town with Westhorpe estate and Little Marlow village remained. So great did the weight of traffic become that less than ten years later it was necessary to bridge the route. A firm trading on Globe Park paid for the work to be done.

Long before motor transport, Marlow was connected to the outside world with the arrival of the Great Marlow Railway Company in 1872. Steam trains served Marlow well for over a century, bringing in coal and other goods. The coal wharves where the old station used to be still remain.

Passenger services were run strictly to timetable. 'The Marlow Donkey', as it was dubbed by the locals, ran regularly between Bourne End and Marlow, occasionally travelling to Maidenhead, High Wycombe and Princes Risborough.

In midwinter, when Old Father Thames burst his banks and flood water frequently lapped the permanent way between Marlow and Bourne End, there was naturally concern among staff and passengers. But the 'Donkey' always got through.

The last steam locomotive to haul the Marlow Donkey was retired to the Dart Valley Railway. In 1972, to mark the 100 years of the line, the former Great Western and British Railways no. 1450, The Centenarian, returned to take part in the celebrations.

By that time there was nothing left of the old railway station, however. Demolition took place in the early 1960s to make way for the development of Marlow industrial estate.

The beloved steam trains were replaced with self-contained diesel-engined carriages in the 1970s. Initially there were two units, but as the demands of the commuting public increased, so did the size of the trains.

A very popular form of transport for pubs and works outings was the motor coach. This group of happy chaps are all set for a day at the seaside in post-war Britain. Most of them pictured here were employees of Y.J. Lovell, the Marlow building company based in premises off Marlow High Street.

In the aftermath of the First World War, Marlow folk wanted a bit of fun for a change. Days out in charabancs were planned on most summer weekends. These employees of Lovell's in 1921 seemed happy enough at the prospect of a drive, but at 12 miles an hour? And what would happen if it rained?

Lovell's had a great record of employee loyalty. There was plenty of banter and laughs from the joinery works and stores at the rear of High Street, reached through an archway where a supermarket now stands. Leonard Galpine (left) was joinery foreman for many years and is seen on his retirement, receiving a gold watch from the company chairman, Peter Lovell, in 1960. Mr Lovell was a direct descendant of Young James Lovell, a Dorset man who founded the company after forming a partnership with two Marlow carpentry and bricklaying firms.

The power of the Thames had long attracted millers to the river banks. There are records of such industry in the Marlow entry of the Domesday Book. Down the centuries many enterprises were established at Marlow, and up until the late 1930s one paper mill was still working.

During the Second World War and in the years immediately after, one relic was used for the storage of a wide range of goods and materials. In the 1960s the mill was burned down, the site cleared and homes built on it.

Following the burning down of the last surviving Marlow mill, plans were made in 1960 for high-class detached houses on the site. But authority decreed the mills should be replaced by something that looked like industrial buildings! That is why these Marlow flats look the way they do.

Mr and Mrs Dereford of Crown Lane devised a system of mosaic art based on the manner in which Aztecs decorated their victim's remains. Their work went on to decorate many buildings in the country including the frontage of a London theatre, a shop in Exeter, an RAF station and this massive collage that embellished the entrance hall of Leicester Forest (East) service station on the M1.

There were many forms of personal transport around at the turn of the century. This horse and carriage, however, was always in great demand, carrying fares to the railway station or meeting them there and transporting them to the various hotels in town.

The horseless carriage began to make its appearance just before the outbreak of the First World War. The licensee of the Red Lion in West Street was not slow to realize the value of a car-hire business.

The Tillion family of Sandygates, off Seymour Court Road, ran a highly successful haulage business in the years between the wars. After the Second World War the firm was nationalized. Their waggons operated from a yard at the rear of The Horns pub in Chapel Street, and a compound behind the converted Ebenezer Chapel in Dean Street.

Another successful haulage firm was G.H. Dean (Marlow) Limited. George (left) and his brother Dennis continued running the firm founded by their father that operated out of a yard in Little Marlow Road. For years they fulfilled a contract for Jackson's Mill in Bourne End, running car components to Dagenham and the Midlands. Dennis ran the coal business of W.T. Porter and Son from an office in Station Approach and the coal wharves and yard nearby.

One of Marlow's most successful businesses was founded in the 1930s by Mr 'Reg' Platt (centre). He opened a garage with a Morris agency and worked out of Quoiting Square and Oxford Road. He also had a radio, TV and electrical shop. His son Jim (right) is now managing director of the garage company. Jim was lucky to survive a potentially fatal incident in July 1944. While visiting his grandmother at Bovingdon Green, a V1 'doodlebug' flying bomb struck a tree nearby. Jim, a lad of ten, was in the garden and showered with fragments. He was severely injured but survived.

Lloyds Bank was the oldest bank in Marlow – the Trustee Savings, National Westminster and National Provincial following much later and Barclays not until the 1960s. Lloyds staff pictured here, just before the outbreak of the Second World War, include Tommy Dunham who lived in Claremont Road, Mont Court of Portland Gardens, Miss Hetty Dumper, who lived in a cottage on The Causeway, and 'Herbie' Habgood of Claremont Gardens, in the back row. Enid Exall is sitting on the right of the manager, Theodore Blatchford.

Above: Coster & Son recently notched up 100 years of trading in Marlow. Alan Coster, the present head of the firm, has a remarkable record of public service. He was the founder secretary of Marlow Chamber of Trade. His other interests have included Marlow Rotary Club, the LVA, of which both he has been president, Marlow Darts League and Marlow Regatta.

Right: The first record of the Coster family in the area was of 'Ted' Coster. He was lock-keeper at Marlow in 1822. His son Edmond, pictured here, started a grocery business at 50 High Street. Eventually the tobacconist's firm, now run by Alan, was founded in 1931 by his father, Sydney, at 52 High Street. A brilliant goalkeeper with Marlow and Bucks hockey team, Sydney died on the field in 1944.

Marlow Chamber of Trade met each month at The Chequers in the High Street in the 1960s and 1970s. When the lady licensee, Mrs Mary Hussey, retired, Jack Bootiman (left), president and manager of the National Provincial Bank, presented her with a set of crystal glasses on behalf of the Chamber. Treasurer Rex Burnett, manager of Westminster Bank, Mrs Leslie Gerrans, assistant secretary, and secretary Alan Carlton look on.

Following Marlow Urban Council's lead to back the town-twinning scheme, the Chamber of Trade made a visit to Marly-le-Roi in 1973. The French equivalent responded with a visit to Marlow the following year. George Wells (right), president of Marlow, and his wife (second from left), welcomed Monsieur Antoine Hertz, president of the French traders' union, and his wife to Marlow.

PLAYERS' PARADISE

Sport and drama have always played a prominent part in the life of Marlow. The soccer and rowing clubs are among the oldest in the country and a very wide cross-section of other sporting clubs exist, all with their own well-appointed facilities. One of the biggest surprises of success came when Chris Baker won the Devizes to Westminster Canoe Race in 1971. He partnered Lawler of Richmond to win in a record time of 19 hours 22 minutes and was included in British Olympic squads of 1972 and 1976. Local drama groups always receive support for their productions. They had to soldier on bravely down the years in average accommodation at Liston Hall and local schools until the Shelley Theatre was built.

These disused gravel pits seen from Winter Hill in 1955 led to a dream project being advanced by Charles Rowe, secretary to Thames Amateur Rowing Council. He wanted to link up the pits on the floor of the valley between Fieldhouse Lane and Little Marlow to result in an international standard 2,000-metre

Mr Rowe is standing behind the Chairman of Marlow UDC, Brooke Furmston, whose wife presented the prizes at the June 1966 Marlow Regatta. It was his last regatta as secretary but he was president of the event the following year.

rowing course. This was many years before the national water sports centre at Holme Pierrepont in Nottinghamshire was ever thought of! His highly advanced ideas were rejected on financial grounds and the inability of the roads in the area to cope with possible large crowds at international events.

Some water sports developed years later at Westhorpe Farm when the Randall family supported water and jet skiing, sailboarding and angling – all in relatively peaceful surroundings.

The arrival of new boats is always an exciting event at any rowing club. On a bright Sunday morning in 1969 one sculling boat, a four, a double sculling pair and training 'tub' were all presented by various donors and named in the traditional fashion. The 'tub' was named after one of the club's most popular characters, A.E. ('Dick') Simpson, who did the honours in person.

Mr Simpson was the head of a printing business off High Street and for years he provided high-quality colour printing to many international film companies. He loved London and nothing gave him greater pleasure than to go to Wardour Street and discuss publicity material for new films. A brilliant after-dinner speaker, Dick, who had an almost endless repertoire of stories and jokes, was in great demand at club suppers.

Steve Redgrave, four times winner of Olympic gold and soon to be seeking a fifth in Sydney, started his rowing career with Great Marlow School in Bobmore Lane. Even in 1977/8 Steve, second from the right, was head and shoulders above the rest of the four, whose success may be judged by the mass of silverware.

Alfred Davis was an incredibly dynamic personality. His career as a professional journalist spanned fifty years. He was a member of the original Marlow Urban Council in 1896 and was chairman four times. His sporting activities brought him even more acclaim as he served Marlow Amateur Regatta as secretary from 1892 until he died in 1924. He also served in various capacities on Marlow Football Club board and had the Oak Tree Road ground named after him in 1928 – four years after his death.

Michael Spracklen and Geoffrey Baker were the first members of Marlow Rowing Club to attain international fame. In the double-sculls event at Lake Padarn in the 1958 Commonwealth Games they achieved a gold medal. The Duke of Edinburgh made the presentation. Mike Spracklen later launched himself on a highly successful international career as a rowing coach.

To mark the centenary of Marlow Rowing Club in 1971 an appeal for £20,000 was launched to double the size of the boathouse and its social facilities. A lot of hard work went into raising the necessary money and in 1975 the new quarters (being on the Berkshire side) were officially opened by Councillor Kit Aston (right), chairman of the newly formed Royal Borough of Windsor and Maidenhead.

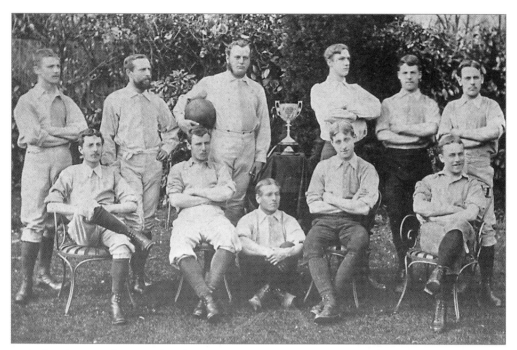

Formed in 1870, Marlow Football Club contributed to the original FA Cup trophy and have never missed an entry for the competition since. In 1881/2 they reached the semifinal with most of the players in this side. They won the Berks & Bucks Cup eleven times before the turn of the century.

After 1900 success was a bit thin on the ground for Marlow until they won the Spartan League, Division 1 championship in 1929/30. This squad of players included many future chairmen and presidents of the club. In the 1937/8 season Marlow won Division 1 of the Spartan League. The past fifty years have seen the demise of amateurism, the selling off of land around the ground and some limited successes. Back row, left to right: George White, Tommy Smith, Bill Slade, Ernest Woodley, Jack Shaw, ? Carter, Herbert Swadling. Second row: Charles Rowe, George Wood, Keith Perfect, Freddie Todd, Ted Cam, Arthur Wood, Billy Perfect, -?-, Bill Oram, Fred Price, Fred Allen, Alfred Jeffreys, 'Tut' Todd. Third row: ? Harvey, Frank Price, Frank Mitchell, Fred Todd, Arthur Mitchell, Mr Llewelyn Shone (president), Frank Peddle, Reg Rockell, Geoff Smith, Jimmy Lovegrove. Front row: Gilbert Price, Percy Roberts, Pat Ryan, Frank Edmonds, Bert Bailey, Mick Walsh, George Bell.

With 100 years of football behind them Marlow FC pushed the boat out in 1970 to contact as many of their former players as they could to celebrate their centenary. Seated at the front, left to right are: 'Herbie' Swadling, president, Bill Oram, Mrs Swadling, Arthur Coventry, Jack Brooks. Middle row: Arthur Mitchell, Frank McKeown, Wilf Keen, -?-, Sammy Gee, Bert Rixon, Mick Walsh, Bill Reeves, Councillor Furmston, -?-, Frank Edmonds. The four standing at the back are George Bryant, Norman Austin, -?-, Billy Dean.

Later in the year a celebration centenary dinner took place at the Compleat Angler Hotel. It was attended by representatives of the Football Association, the Berks and Bucks FA, as well as trustees, civic guests, club officers and players.

In the days when England had an amateur international side their inspiration, coach and mentor was Dr Charles Hughes (in the middle wearing the dark track suit). Training for one of their last encounters as amateurs, this England squad turned out on Marlow's Alfred Davis Memorial Ground in the mid-1960s. 'Charlie' had requested special permission from Marlow, as he considered the Bisham Abbey ground 'unsuitable'.

There was a highly professional squad gracing the Alfred Davis pitch one Sunday afternoon in 1979. Rick Wakeman, pop star and keyboard wizard, arranged for two teams to play for charity. In front of a crowd of thousands George Best, standing fifth from left, kicked off. Involved were many disc jockeys, pop stars, musicians and footballers.

Floodlit rugby came to Marlow on a bitterly cold night in November 1973 when there was a match between the home side (in the dark shirts with white hoops) against referee Mike Titcomb's international XV. Bill Murphy, president of the Marlow club, is standing on the right.

'Catch 'em young' was the Marlow policy when they were the first club in the country to start mini-rugby in 1970. Ever since then, a well-patronized tournament has taken place once a year at Riverwoods, taking entries from all over England and Wales.

Before the British Lions left for their South African tour in 1974 a party to wish them well was arranged by Marlow Rugby Club president, Bill Murphy (second from right), and Irish Internationalist, Willie John McBride (eighth from left). Both men had connections with Black Rock club in Dublin and Bill arranged for the two big lion mascots to accompany the group on tour.

Marlow Hockey Club was formed in 1907 and became a founder member of the Sports Club in 1949. Many distinguished players have been members, but the one international, however, played for Scotland – Robin Laird (fourth from right).

Marlow Bowling Club began seventy-five years ago at the rear of the Crown Hotel then moved to Higginson Park. It has a remarkable record in the Bucks Cup. John Lewis, Ian Harvey and Arthur Plestedd, seen here, won the English Bowling Association triples in 1971. John Lewis died later and is remembered in a charity competition each August.

Celebrations with good reason in 1972 at the 50th anniversary of the club. Marlow Bowls Club members proudly show off their trophies. On the top left is Aubrey Maynard and at the back is John Henniker. The next four down, left to right, are Harry Price, Charlie Sparks, Ian Harvey and Len Goodway. George Morton is on the left at the front, with Wally Griffin, and Arthur Britnell is in the centre. The three at the bottom right are Bill House, Bill Wing and Claude Highfield.

The national press were scouring London one Saturday night in 1967 looking for Mike Keen and the League Cup. He had captained Queen's Park Rangers to the first Wembley victory over West Bromich Albion. The competition was a 'cinderella' to begin with, being boycotted by the league's big guns, but Wembley gave it status after this day. A former Marlow Park cricketer, Mike was attending the club's annual dinner at the George & Dragon.

Marlow Racing Pigeon Club is proud of a large membership, built up over many years. It is also their boast that they have more trophies than Marlow Regatta. This group was attending the annual dinner in the George and Dragon in 1963. The chairman, Bill Edwards, is fourth from the left and behind him is Dennis Dean, club president at that time.

Marlow Angling Club was founded in 1937 by a former mayor of Henley, Fred Butler (third from left). He was first chairman and then was made president in 1960 after twenty-five years' service. A professional sign-writer, he lost a leg in the First World War but this did not prevent him scaling ladders over many Marlow shop fronts.

Many thousands of children within the scouting movement have visited Longridge in Quarry Wood Road, Bisham, in the past forty years. The former large house and grounds is now operated by the Scout Association as the national water sports centre. It is one of only two, the other being at Kielder Forest, Northumberland. In addition to canoeing, sailing is also taught and it provides a camping venue for scouts, guides and other youth organizations.

Marlow has many scout and cub scout troops and packs. Each one has had problems with accommodation and finding responsible adults to take charge of proceedings. Akela Mrs Shelly was one of the longer serving leaders until she and her family moved away. She is seen briefing Marlow cub scouts before a St George's Day parade.

In 1957 Marlow Boxing Club was formed by local businessman, Alan McLachlan. Based at first in The Armoury, Institute Road, the club moved to Court Garden where successful tournaments were staged. After one event in 1963, John Lowe (left), president, presented prizes to Jack Wilson, club light-heavyweight champion and future club trainer and Gary Ansell, best schoolboy. Club chairman Arthur Brown (right) was a former Bucks Special Constabulary inspector, and is now nationally involved with the Burma Star Association; he is Parade Marshal at Marlow's annual Remembrance Sunday services.

Marlow Football Club regularly changes officials. John Weaver (centre) gave up as coach/manager in 1974. John Fisher (left), a former Marlow centre-half who played for Wycombe Wanderers and Wales Amateur XI, took over and was welcomed by Marlow's chairman Reg Seymour, himself later to be president.

Marlow Amateur Operatic Society was formed in 1926. The first production staged was *HMS Pinafore* by Gilbert and Sullivan in Liston Hall. It was the forerunner of many more shows until the Second World War affected schedules.

The society was reformed in 1955 and their first show in 1956 – thirty years on – was *HMS Pinafore*! The Liston Hall venue was still favourite as Marlow Players' studio was adjacent and was pressed into service on occasions as dressing rooms.

Still with the Operatic Society, the leading ladies in *Iolanthe* strove to overcome the dressing room blues . . . and succeeded!

When the Shelley Theatre in Court Gardens became available in 1975, some players had difficulty adjusting to the 'demountable' stage. Sections were built up to form the central platform and several actors fell over the back. The dressing accommodation in the bowels of the old building left much to be desired originally. The men's chorus of *Iolanthe* bravely prepare for their entrance.

The 'youngest' of Marlow's drama groups, The Entertainers, was formed in 1963. Soon after that these members went to Maidenhead Festival and came away with the top trophy for best all-female production. Back row, left to right: Fee Murch, Joyce Newman, Phyllis Blanche, Shirley Large and Gay Newman. Front row: Pauline Hurst, Joyce Windridge, Joan Tandy and Joan Hurst.

The world of speedboat racing was stunned when Ronnie Watts (left) and Paul Yeoman won the diesel-engined section of the *Daily Express* Power Boat Race from Cowes to Weymouth in 1962/3. They were aboard *The Lesser Nit*, a 23-ft Fairey Huntress hulled craft powered by a turbo-charged 6-cylinder, 145 h.p. Perkins diesel engine. Brian Folley supervised the construction and fitting out at Harleyford, upstream from Marlow.

The oldest drama group in Marlow was started up sixty years ago. Their productions were mostly presented in Liston Hall until Shelley Theatre became available. The members have always entered wholeheartedly into local affairs. This picture shows them preparing their float to tour the main streets of the town in the Marlow Carnival.

The original Marlow Cricket Club was founded in 1829, but has had a chequered history. The present club is an offshoot of Marlow Sports Club founded in October 1949, with three sections – rugby, hockey and cricket. These Edwardian chaps had just engaged in a cricket match between the club and Marlow Institute and are posing on the steps of the pavilion, built in the last century.

The original pavilion still stands. At one time the rugby club had a large building adjacent. In the 1960s this was demolished when the rugger men went their own way. Now this two-storey dressing room and function accommodation has replaced it. The new sports club pavilion was built in 1972–3.

ROUND & ABOUT

Marlow has nine near neighbours, two of them across the Thames in Berkshire. In less enlightened times Marlow and Marlow Bottom could have become one unit but successive planning authorities have frowned on this. The bypass seems to have ruled out any merging with Little Marlow but it is not difficult to visualize a link-up with Bovingdon Green and Marlow Common in the long term. In 'The Valley', as Marlow Bottom residents refer to their area, parish councillors joined forces with local residents in a war against litterbugs in 1972.

To the west of the main Lane End Road lies Widmere Farm. This perfectly preserved building is believed to have been built by the Knights Templars who had property at Bisham as well. They are also credited with building the first bridge over the Thames to connect their holdings.

Booker aerodrome was the site of filming for much of *Those Magnificent Men in their Flying Machines*, where a replica of Brooklands was constructed. Many strange shapes took to the air on the end of crane jibs. After the real filming finished bandleader Billy Cotton arrived with his crew and did their spoof version of things. The result was televised on the *Billy Cotton Bandshow*.

There are many secluded homes in the Marlow Common area to the north-west of Marlow. This unusual house was known originally as Monk's Corner, but after associations with Jerome K. Jerome it became known as Jerome Cottage.

The Royal Oak pub is a popular watering hole today. In 1902 it was patronized by as many horses as customers. The pond was one of a chain throughout the country in the days when the horse was king and lorries had not even been thought of. One licensee called Church came from the Channel Islands to run the Oak, and three of his children attended Bovingdon Green School in Spinfield Lane.

Roughly two miles upstream from Marlow is Temple Lock. At one time a ferry made it possible to walk all the way to Henley on the old towpath, but the Second World War ended that. Just a few yards downstream stake boats moor for the starting point of races in Marlow Regatta each year.

Ramblers and walkers pressed for years to have the link between Marlow and Henley restored. Eventually this footbridge that allows for navigation was built. On completion it was the last link in the Thames Walk from Lechlade to the Thames Barrier.

Harleyford Manor dominates the Thames between Temple and Hurley Locks. This vast structure, recently restored to its former opulence, was the seat of the powerful Clayton family for many years. Like a great many other big houses in the Thames Valley, it was said to be the model for Toad Hall in *The Wind in the Willows* by Kenneth Grahame.

Midway between Marlow and Henley lies Medmenham, famous for a Viking encampment on the escarpment at Danesfield. The parish church congregation annually held a big fête in the Vicarage garden to raise funds. The Hellfire Club from West Wycombe, led by Sir Frances Dashwood, is believed to have had sinister connections with Medmenham Abbey.

Little Marlow village dates back to the twelfth century which was when the parish church was built. Many people commute to large towns and cities to work but prefer the quiet country life of this village. Massive market garden and gravel pit enterprises surround the village. Edgar Wallace, the crime writer and novelist, attended church here regularly but he is not buried in the churchyard. His grave is in Little Marlow Cemetery, about half a mile towards Bourne End.

A regular feature of August Bank Holiday Monday in the village is the annual fête, when funds are raised for sporting and local amenities. The committee try to have a special feature each year. In 1973 it was the turn of the Morris Men from Datchet.

Wayside Cottages at Bisham featured on a commercial postcard soon after the end of the First World War. The idyllic scene includes a resident hanging out her washing on the green in front of the ivy-covered homes, all in the shade of an avenue of mature trees.

In 1972, soon after the opening of the A404 Marlow–Bisham bypass, the contractors created a spur road leading to the dual carriageway just round the corner. No further comment is required!

A massive multi-million-pound sports complex was built in the grounds of historic Bisham Abbey between 1967 and 1969. In addition to this building floodlit all-weather outdoor tennis courts were laid out. Tim Henman from Maidenhead is a product of this facility.

The main building of the twelfth-century Bisham Abbey is relatively well preserved. It contains administration offices and dormitories for visiting sportspeople.

Above: During a Royal Progress down the
River Thames in October 1974, the Queen
landed at Bisham Abbey. Despite a wet and
miserable day Her Majesty insisted on walking
round all the Sports Council facilities. She was
accompanied by the manager of Bisham, Brian
Lee (right). The England international soccer
team now trains there regularly.

Right: Sporting connections at Bisham Abbey
started with the Central Council for Physical
Recreation after the Second World War. Much
amused confusion arose when British athletes
appeared with 'CCPR' logos and were
mistaken for Russians. In 1956 the Duke of
Edinburgh, piloting a Royal Navy Whirlwind
helicopter, landed in the grounds. During the
walkabout His Royal Highness noticed dew-
laden spiders' webs in the corner of exercise
bars and quipped, 'You don't have many
gymnasts here, then'.

ACKNOWLEDGEMENTS

My grateful thanks are extended to a host of friends and acquaintances in Marlow without whose help this book would not have been possible. Firstly to Mrs Gil Anderson for the superb cover photograph and Mrs Anne Hobbs for the 1915 munitions workers on the back. Many of the photographs were the work of my very good pal, the late Alan Holmes. I hope this work will give some testimony to his craft and thanks are due to his widow Pauline for giving her permission to use them.

Still on the photography front Joe Green has my eternal gratitude for his patience and brilliant darkroom work; also my former colleagues Harold Fletcher, Geoff Gomm, Bob Mead and Ron Goodearl for use of their pictures.

The following people were also pleased to assist me: Mrs Edna Berry, Mrs Audrey Dorsett, Mrs Christine Harding, Miss Louise Charrison, Mrs May Derham, Mrs D. Simpson, Miss M.E. Griffin, Mrs Kath Page, Mrs R. Harvey, Mrs B.S.J. Sheppard, Mrs F. Edmonds, Mrs E.A.B. Orr, Mrs Wendy Ball, Mrs Doreen Price, Mrs Susan Fanning, Bill Henns, Arthur Woolford, Charles Towers, Leslie C.W. White, Francis Smith, Ted Sturt, Ken Drucquer, Ted Sewell, Alan Coster, Eric Burger and Messrs Broad & Gloyens.